MW00897137

Printed in The United States of America.

shanaolmstead.com

ISBN: 9798359255509

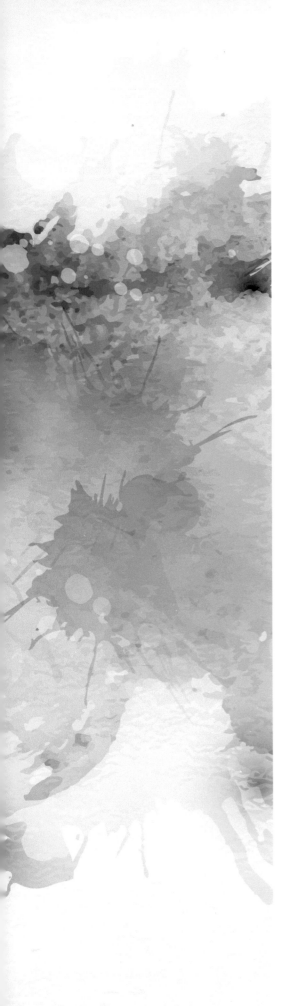

Contents

4th Chakra

5th Chakra

6th Chakra

7th Chakra

Integration After Awakening

Wrapping Up

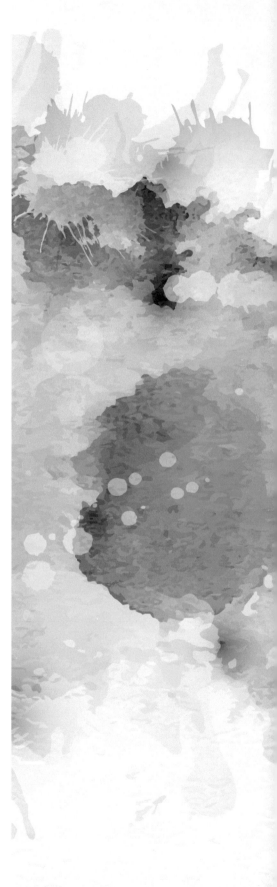

BEFORE WE BEGIN

As a sensitive empathic being, you are on the leading edge
of consciousness.

As you awaken and evolve, you assist the rest of humanity
to evolve as well.

We are moving towards more and more souls awakening
to their spiritual truth, you are here to help with this global
evolutionary awakening!

Introduction

Tuning into your empathic superpower

If you identify as a highly sensitive person, or empath, congratulations!

You are in the approximately 20% of the population that feels things deeply, that can feel others emotions, and are very sensitive and intuitive, and can naturally sense divine source energy.

We will work through how to accept and embrace this beautiful sensitivity and learn to channel it as the superpower it truly is!

Tuning into your intuition as an empath

We are all born with a powerful intuitive knowing. Especially for empathic people, we have access to a powerful source of knowledge, much more accurate that our brains will ever be.

We also tend to doubt ourselves, be self critical, and too worried about other people to hear the magical inner wisdom.

This book is here to help you create the space you need, and the tools to help guide your towards your own amazing inner knowing!

Healing old wounds

We all have old subconscious beliefs and wounds that impede our growth and our belief in the magnificent potential we all have.

If we don't work through these, they end up running our life and limiting us.

Unhealed wounds and trauma trigger our nervous system to activate the stress responses of fight, flight, freeze or fawn.

We will look together at some of the history that is still active in you and learn tools to keep your nervous system more regulated so that you can hear your unique and powerful truth.

Understanding your true purpose

If you are still operating in the old paradigm of fear disconnection, there is no way to have clarity on why you chose to incarnate this time around.

When you can truly feel your intuition, and have worked through some old wounding, you will be able to have more awareness of your true natural gifts and talents that will lead you to your purpose in the world.

We will work through practices to help you hear more clearly your inner truth that has always been there guiding you towards your highest path.

As you embrace your empathic gifts, understand your intuition, feel safer in your body and know your path, you feel more alive and aware than ever before. You see things more clearly, and you are excited to share your gifts with others.

You are in the process of spiritual awakening!

A LITTLE MORE ABOUT ME

I am a Spiritual Psychotherapist and have been inspired by my own journey of awakening to help others awaken to their own spiritual nature.

My spiritual connection has been completely life changing, and allowed me to move through challenges in my life while remaining solidly connected to feeling the loving support of the Universe. I have helped many people awaken, and move forward on their path of spiritual connection.

My intention for this collection of my writings is to help spark the light of awareness in you, and to be a comforting guide on your spiritual journey.

chapter one

Spiritual Awakening & Transformation

What is a spiritual awakening?

In my experience and those that I've known and worked with, it is a transformation. A waking up to a new belief system and energetic experience of the world.

It is a feeling that everything is the same, but also somehow very different. The events in life seem to take on a different meaning and life is richer and more colorful.

It often takes getting to a place of extreme pain, through crisis, death or some other event that helps us shift our old ego based ways of seeing the world. At these points in time it is easier to cut through the veil and feel enlightened energy opening us up to the truth. This can feel like a brand new way of seeing the world while at the same time feeling totally familiar in a way we can't really explain.

It feels so familiar, because we come here knowing all of these spiritual truths. We are born knowing we are beings of light, here to spread and expand love and compassion. We are born understanding that we are all one, and completely connected. We are born knowing that there is no separation, and fear is an illusion. That everything, including us, is made of energy. That we have lessons we want to learn and choose experiences to allow us to learn them in order to increase our consciousness.

That's why many times a spiritual awakening can feel like coming home, because it is. We are meant to feel connected to something bigger than us, to feel a sense of meaning, passion, connection and fulfillment. If you are not feeling this way, it's ok, it just means there is some work for you to do in order to allow the connection with this, because it's meant for you and everyone to connect to.

In more practical everyday awakening terms, let's break down this whole spiritual awakening concept. My terminology doesn't have to be yours. There are lots of other words or ways to explain this experience: mid-life or quarter life crisis, nervous breakdown, transformation, hitting rock bottom, changing your life, waking up, etc.....For me personally, spiritual awakening is what resonates because they are the words that came to me during my own experience of waking up.

Since my own spiritual awakening experience over 15 years ago, I have felt a calling to study this process. I love to guide others and help to increase and validate the beginning sparks of awareness, and then to be a loving and experienced guide in helping them to navigate the feelings and life changes that often accompany the major spiritual awakening that follows. It is so super exciting to witness someone's total transformation in consciousness, and know the ripple effect this will be creating on the world around them.

I have noticed through my years of experience in this area that there are certain stages that are similar in people's experiences. It is my hope that this book will help you to understand and make sense of whatever stage you are in, and help you continue to move forward in your evolution with calm and joy!

The Stages of a Spiritual Awakening

Living unconsciously:

This means just living life, probably with a sense of something missing but having no idea what or how to fix it. Not being very aware of what you are really feeling or what you really want. Sometimes feeling anxious or depressed or like you're living on the surface of life. Some people live their whole lives in this state and that's ok.

Breakdown:

This is when, usually predicated by one big crisis, or several smaller ones over months or years, you reach the end of feeling like you have control over your life or your happiness. You don't know what to do next, but you know things can't go on the way they are.

Letting go:

When nothing you know is working anymore and the realization that you really don't have control settles in. This can feel real scary at first, but the beautiful thing is that none of us ever really have control, and this awareness is ultimately magical and freeing. It allows us to move on to the next steps of awakening and trusting the universe.

Spark of Awakening:

After realizing we don't really have control, there begins to be a spark of awareness and curiosity about other ways to see the world. Often people begin practices that they have never done before in this lifetime, but that their soul recognizes as essential for their continued evolution.

Things like: meditation, yoga, being in nature more, prayer, affirmations, reading spiritual

or inspirational texts, learning more about religious or metaphysical or energetic traditions, taking spiritual classes and workshops, journaling, etc. These practices all get us ready for connecting more deeply with ourselves and the next steps in our awakening process.

Redefining self:

As we continue to be consciously or unconsciously drawn through these stages of waking up, our sense of ourselves begins shifting. We begin redefining who we think we are: a student, a CEO, a mother, an accountant, etc…. and begin to understand the expansiveness of our potential a little bit.

Our consciousness only allows us to know what we are ready for, in order to help us move forward without overwhelming us with perceived pressure to be as magnificent as the universe knows we truly are.

Big time spiritual download and awakening:

At this point there is often a bigger and more intense increase in consciousness. Things like manifesting and co-creating our reality begin to make more sense. Big ideas that may have just seemed like cheesy statements in the past truly are integrated into your awareness now: things like "we are all one," "love is all there is," "everything is connected," and "we are spiritual beings having a human experience". Instead of just seeing or saying these things you start really feeling them down to your bones and living your life in accordance with these principles.

You begin to understand that we are meant to love ourselves as creation does, and that helps everyone around us. You know now that as your own consciousness increases, your light shines brighter, giving all around you permission to do the same. You start to understand that we are all powerful souls and are choosing our life experiences to learn to grow. You really let go and trust the universe to help your path unfold towards your highest good. You really really want to find your "purpose" in order to help the world.

Finding purpose:

Often at this point, the process of awakening feels so good to your energy system and your frequency is so elevated that steps towards your purpose begin to become clearer to you. You start to recognize that finding your soul's purpose is actually pretty easy. Once you can learn to be more consistently out of your fear based ego and follow the path of joy instead, the next steps continue to be lit up much more clearly for you. Your purpose is always down the path of joy.

Spiritual community:

So many people get so excited at this stage of awakening that they try to get everyone around them to get on board. I have seen many examples of wives wanting to wake up their husbands, or friends wanting their friends to understand their new ideas, or daughters wanting their moms to increase their consciousness to match their own new level of awareness.

I truly understand this because I felt the same way. I was so excited about my new way of being I tried to help all the people in my life get it too. As empaths, we are naturally drawn to helping people, but often people in our lives aren't at the same place in consciousness as we are and are not ready or willing to change. As we learn to let go of that desire, and focus back on our own spiritual growth (or get into a super fun job like I did where I get to do this all day every day!) we accelerate our own process and let the souls of those around us evolve when and how is right for them, not us.

We begin to see the wounds and issues of our family of origin in a different way, and are able to forgive and accept those in our history who we perceive as hurting us, and understand it only came from their own lack of consciousness.
We begin to filter those out around us who are negative or unconscious, and begin to require that our days are filled with only conscious and positive people in our lives. It's so important as we continue our growth that we have soul tribe members around us who are growing too, this helps all of us expand.

Understanding energy:

As we evolve we generally begin to be more aware and sensitive to our own energy and that of those around us, our environments, and what we put in and on our bodies.

It is usually a natural progression for those who are becoming more aware to begin shifting into workplaces and family situations that are more in alignment with their new consciousness. This sensitivity also helps us to create more peaceful environments to live and work in, and to pay more attention to the energy of the food we eat and toxicity levels of everything around them.

Spiritual practice:

In order to maintain the amazing magical feeling of a spiritual awakening forever it is so important to integrate spiritual practice into your life. Not just once a week at yoga class (which is also great!) but I'm talking about all day every day. The most amazing spiritual teachers didn't just do a lot of inner spiritual work and then are able to coast the rest of their lives, no, they continue, every day, for the rest of their lives to practice remembering.

We are all still human, and our cute little human brains will always have things to say that aren't true, so it's up to us to consistently bring in things that help us remember that we are all beautiful magical pieces of the divine. That there is nothing to fear at all ever. That we all chose all of this and are always surrounded by loving energy more powerful than we can imagine. That we are magnificent and powerful souls.

Everyone is unique and has practices that are best suited for their own evolution, but some consistent practices that I have seen that really work are:

- Meditation
- Prayer
- Yoga
- Being in spiritual community
- Affirmations
- Gratitude
- Consistent awareness of thought and feelings
- Self-love all day every day (internal self-loving dialogue, external self-loving acts)
- Reading and listening to things that inspire you
- Being in nature
- Journaling
- Being quiet and still

Spiritual awakening does not go backwards, and awareness cannot be erased, just remember it is your natural state. Relaxing, getting out of the way, and allowing divine wisdom to flow through you and guide you is the most effective way to awaken and continue to grow. Follow your joy and have fun!

These stages are not exact, and can come in different forms and orders, this is just a general outline from what I have observed and experienced over the years. There is no right or wrong way to evolve.

The next chapters will walk you through a process to become more aligned with your true spiritual nature. To help you to spiritually awaken and integrate these new awarenesses into your life permanently!

We will work through the Chakra system to illustrate a process of using practical magic to evolve your spiritual nature.

chapter two

Taking Space

Taking Space

It's so much harder to connect to the spiritual truth of who you are if you don't have the space in your life to connect with yourself.

Empaths need space away from other people to hear their intuition.

When our nervous system is overstimulated, we are not ourselves and not in touch with our own intuitive guidance.

The Universe is always working on communicating with you, to guide and help, we just have too much resistance usually to hear it.

You are the foundation for the rest of your life, you deserve and need this space. When I began meditating, and really listening to myself, my life transformed.

It's always best to proactively create space for yourself, and if you don't plug this in, you may notice some of these signs that you haven't given yourself enough space.

To connect spiritually, it's very important to have a lot of quiet space to assist in your awakening of consciousness. Another term for this that I like is Alonliness. The feeling of missing yourself, having too many distractions/stimulations to hear your own inner voice.

Signs That You Need Space

Irritability:

One of the first signs of Alonliness is being irritable. This can happen with anyone in your life, even those people you really like hanging out with. It's not something to judge yourself for, it's just a sign that you may need more time to be quiet and recharge by yourself.

Confusion:

Sensitive people like you need space to know how you think and feel. Another sign of alonliness is feeling confused, not knowing what to do or how you feel. In order to gain more clarity, it's important to spend time connecting your energy back with yourself, and unhooking from others.

Low Energy:

This one took me a while to learn. I realized that when my energy is low, it doesn't mean there's anything wrong, sometimes I just need a little time alone.

For empaths, our energy system is often unconsciously plugging in to others around us. We are attuning to them, making sure everything is harmonious. While this is easy for us, we also need some time to unplug from others, and plug into ourselves and the universe to fill back up with energy!

When you notice any of these signs, stop, take a deep breath and remind yourself that you are worth taking space for. That the world needs you to operate at your highest capacity so that you can bring your gifts to the world.

Ways to Make Sure You Have The Space You Need:

Be Honest With Yourself:

If you're feeling some of the signs above, it's important to stop pretending you're not.

It's ok to need some time away, so don't judge yourself for this.

It's so important to not try to be like "everyone else" and accept that you need time alone to feel your best. It is a sign of evolved consciousness to be able to know who you are and what you need.

Tell yourself "In order to be my best I am going to create space to connect with myself."

Set Boundaries:

This is hard sometimes, especially for super nice people like you!

Generally people in your life are willing to respect your boundaries. It's up to you to be honest with yourself to know what they are, and to communicate them with people in your life.

Do some internal reflection to find clarity on what you need, and let others know.

Be confident when you state your needs, and if you encounter any push back from them, you can explain "I am realizing that I have a need to recharge by myself in order to maintain my energy."

Let them know it's not personal, and that you will be a better partner, mother, son, etc., the better you take care of yourself.

Be Consistent:

This is so important! Be proactive and consistent with your energy management practices.

In order to prevent most of the extreme symptoms of alonliness, plug in some alone time into your calendar.

Check in with yourself to see if it's an hour, a day, or longer that you need, and consistently commit to that.

It can be 5 minutes of meditation, or a walk in nature by yourself once a day, or a day by yourself exploring the city once a month.

Make sure you are giving yourself this magical preventative medicine to keep your vibration at a maximum level for you, you deserve it!

What is in the way of me taking the space I need and deserve for myself?

What spiritual gifts will come into my life when I give myself the space I need?

_____
_____
_____
_____
_____
_____
_____
_____
_____
_____
_____
_____
_____
_____
_____
_____
_____
_____
_____

What are 5 ways I will maintain the space I need in my life?

1. _____
2. _____
3. _____
4. _____
5. _____

the sensitive soul's guide to spiritual awakening

affirmation:

"I am worth taking space for."

Repeat this affirmation as much as you can remember throughout the day to help your subatomic particles and subconscious mind believe this beautiful truth.

practice:

Start small, 15 minutes a day.

Get an app, practice on a walk, get more comfortable being quiet and listening to yourself without distraction.

Sensitive people need even more space than others to disconnect from others' energy and tune into their own. You may find you are not anxious or depressed...just overstimulated and/or in environments that are not beneficial for your energetic alignment.

energy tip:

Wherever you are, whatever you're doing, whoever is around you, visualize beautiful space around you. It is just yours, helping you feel joyful, peaceful, and safe. Remind your energy system that you always have this love bubble around you, and energy easily flows through and doesn't affect you.

chapter three

1st Chakra Transcend Your Triggers

1st Chakra Transcend Your Triggers

The first root chakra represents your feeling of belonging and safety in the world.

Empathic people often have a hard time staying grounded and feeling safe in the world.

In order to connect spiritually, we have to feel safe.

Grounding pulling up earth energy is essential to your immune system. Grounding helps you feel safe enough so that your nervous system is out of fight or flight and in the parasympathetic nervous system response instead.

Not feeling safe in your body blocks your intuition and your feeling of spiritual connection.

This naturally allows your old beliefs to transform, to be released.

Understanding ourselves and what our triggers are is important in the process of developing more of a feeling of safety in our bodies.

"Triggers" are anything that create a misalignment in your energy system. That pull you out of the natural, responsive, parasympathetic aspect of your nervous system, into the sympathetic nervous system reaction known as the fight or flight response.

Allow these triggers to be triggers of positive self-care practice. Let them be a reminder to you to give yourself some love and forgiveness. To take some deep breaths and remind yourself "all is well in this moment, I am loved beyond measure."
Rather than bringing you down, stopping your day, and creating negative thought spirals, instead your triggers can be the pathway into

spiritual growth and transcendence.

Your triggers can be your biggest teachers!

Some ways to put this into practice are:

Pay Attention:

Practice mindfulness first. Just practice being a non-judgmental observer to your triggers.

Keep a journal of moments when you notice your energy get tight and constricted. What just happened? What were you thinking and feeling?

Creating awareness of the patterns of your triggers prepares you to begin the process of transforming them into portals to expanded consciousness.

Keep Your Vibe High:

As you start to create awareness of when and how your energy system gets triggered, it's also very important to work on feeling good.

The better you feel the majority of the time, the easier it will be to notice your triggers, and shift them in the moment.
You are building a resilient energy and nervous system that will allow you to quickly bounce back to a frequency of love instead of staying in the negative trigger spiral.

This is a very individualized process, only you know what brings you joy and lifts your frequency, but some necessary ingredients to a consistently high level of energetic vibration are:
  ~ Regular meditation
  ~ Time in Nature
  ~ Positive community
  ~ Thinking positive thoughts
  ~ Frequent joy and laughter!

Bring in the Light:

Once you have established more of an understanding of yourself and your triggers, it's time to start practicing.

One easy way to start is, when you notice your energy constrict, wiggle your toes, and imagine beautiful white light entering your toes from the earth, and gently streaming up through your whole body.

Place your hand on your heart, take three deep breaths and remind your energy system, silently or out loud: "It is safe to expand, I am one with the Universe."

Your energy body just needs some reminders sometimes. It's going through a lot right now, so be kind and tender with yourself as you remind it that it is always safe, and love is all there is.

Remember it's Always About You:

When we get triggered, it's about us.

This doesn't mean that there are not energy vampires out there, and mean people, of course there are!

It does mean that when we feel victimized by someone or something, rather than project the problem onto them, it's an invitation to get curious with yourself instead.

For example, if someone is being mean to you, instead of getting mad at them, ask yourself "What in me believes what they say?" and "How can I be kind and nurturing to myself in this moment, while holding healthy boundaries in this situation?"

The suffering only stays with us if we believe what they are saying. If we know it's not true, we can love ourselves, and still say to the person "I didn't like how that felt."
The more neutral we can be about it, the less suffering happens.

Take it Lightly:

As you move through this process, you will naturally start to see more separation between your thoughts and your consciousness as the observer of these thoughts.

You will begin to see the humor and cuteness of some of these thoughts that you used to take sooo seriously.

You begin to laugh at yourself in a gentle way, beginning to remember that the truth of who you are is never the fear based thoughts that dominate your brain much of the time.

This lightness and humor is a natural part of the evolutionary process, and means you are understanding even more that you are not your thoughts!

the sensitive soul's guide to spiritual awakening

This is one of the beautiful benefits of doing your own inner work. You become so light and peaceful and beautiful, that it helps to shift the vibration of those around you.

You become a part of the global awakening of consciousness on the planet, helping us all to evolve!

This can be a fun practice if you can take it lightly! We are meant to take things lightly, we are here to have fun, spread joy and light and love

Have fun allowing your triggers to transform you!

Allow these triggers to be triggers of positive self-care practice. Let them be a reminder to you to give yourself some love and forgiveness. To take some deep breaths and remind yourself "all is well in this moment, I am loved beyond measure."

When you get triggered, it activates the stress response in the sympathetic aspect of your nervous system.

There are 4 main types of stress/trauma/ trigger responses: Fight, flight, freeze and fawn.

Now that you have more awareness of what triggers you to feel unsafe in your body, we can go a little deeper with a journaling exercise to help you find clarity on your go to response(s) and how they developed.

What is my go-to Stress/Trauma Trigger Response:

Fight: You tend to get defensive, attack, yell, criticize, get angry, nag, etc.

Flight: You stay distracted, busy, escape, feeling trapped, anxiety, etc.

Freeze: You tend towards disassociation, numbing out, feeling heavy, etc.

Fawn: You people please, can be codependent, not stand up for yourself, etc.

Fight

You learned that yelling or fighting back was rewarded in your family, or made the stressful situation stop. You developed this habit, even though now it has a negative impact on you and your relationships, it's hard to stop.

You are just trying to protect yourself and stay safe. You may have had this modeled by a parent. You may have felt misunderstood in your emotions and sensitivity, and were trying to be understood by people that didn't "get" you, or invalidated you.

Flight

You learned that running away, leaving the room or the house, staying very busy and distracted helped you feel less stressed as a child. You may have seen a parent model this behavior, or just felt that there was no other option for you to feel safe because you are so sensitive.

Empaths are very sensitive to energy, you may not have had the words for this as a child, but just needed to be in your own space to feel safe.

Freeze

You learned to shut down in order to feel safe. This can look like hiding in your room, playing 12 hours of video games a day, sleeping a lot, and can sometimes look like depression.

When little sensitive nervous systems are overwhelmed by stress, they want to shut everything out and hide. You may have had a parent modeling this shutting down behavior.

Fawn

You learned to people please, to accommodate, to suppress your own feelings and needs in order to feel safe. You may have had a parent who had strong emotions, and you had to walk on eggshells, or try to be helpful and perfect in order to keep the peace. This may have been reinforced for you, being a "good" girl or boy, and you're soooo nice!

How did this develop in your childhood?

How was it protective for you?

Write a letter from your inner child asking for what you need, that you didn't receive as a child.

Then, write a letter back from adult you, letting him/her know how you are taking care of them now, and they don't need to stay in their stress response anymore, they are safe to be who they are now.

Write down a new belief to practice, the antidote to each stress response:

Fight: "I am you; you are me; we are one"
Flight: "It is safe to be still and in my body"
Freeze: "I approach the world with joyful wonder."
Fawn: "I deserve to take up space in the world."

_____

_____

_____

_____

_____

_____

_____

Write down who you are stepping into and what you must let go of to let it in.
Example: I am expanding into more confidence and safety in my body, I am releasing fear.

_____

_____

_____

_____

_____

_____

_____

practice:

Check ins to ground your energy and remind you of your safety and affirmation multiple times a day.

Reminding yourself frequently of the here and now to stay out of fear

Fear blocks your intuition, so your body must feel safe to hear its internal guidance system.

Notice your stress responses activating, and practice bringing in your new affirmation, feeling it circulating through your body and bringing you safety and peace in every moment.

affirmation:

"Earth energy flows to me effortlessly, bringing me grounding and safety so that I can hear my intuition and feel my spiritual connection."

energy tip:

Opening roots from the bottoms of your feet to pull up energy.

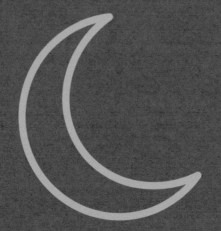

chapter four

2nd Chakra Expand Your Joy

2nd Chakra | Expand Your Joy

The second chakra is your center for creativity, joy, abundance, and your personal emotions.

Now that you are feeling more safe and grounded, and have tools to work through your triggers, you can work on expanding your joy.

This chapter will focus on helping you to maintain a more joyful energetic vibration so that you can continue expanding into your spiritual awakening.

Joy is your birthright and natural state. The more often you can stay in this place, the easier it will be to move through the next steps in the process of expanding your consciousness.

What if all of life is a practice to help you learn how to stay in alignment? What if challenges and irritations are not there to just frustrate you but to actually help you grow and expand? What if your ability to maintain a positive vibration is what really matters most of all? What if our ability to keep our vibration elevated is what is creating our circumstances and future, and the better we feel the better our life will continue to be?

Relaxing into this awareness can be very freeing. There are really no problems to be solved, only circumstances that come up to be aware of and mindfully respond to.

I'm not saying that it's not sometimes a good idea to consider changing our circumstances if they are negative or not serving us. What I am saying is that when we are in situations that we can't change in the moment, we can use them to evolve rather than resist, to grow rather than shut down.

In order to get better at shifting your frequency in more challenging circumstances, it's really helpful to be working on keeping your vibration in a positive place most of the time. This will allow your energy to be expansive in general which makes it easier to bounce back when more difficult things happen.

Vibration is everything. In the words of Nikola Tesla, "If you want to know the secrets of the universe, think in terms of energy, frequency and vibration." If we are not conscious, our vibration can be influenced a lot by external circumstances.

Have you ever noticed your feelings change when you enter certain environments or situations? Or that you feel tired and drained around or after you leave a conversation with someone? Or that you feel peaceful and relaxed on a lovely day at the beach?

We are all impacted to some extent by the world around us. The problem is when we are unaware, especially of the negative energy around us and how it affects us. If we aren't aware of the connection between things around us and our own vibration we can tend to blame ourselves for feelings instead, or feel confused about why we feel the way we do.

Beginning to create more awareness of your own vibration, independent of other people or situations is vital in order to create a baseline for yourself. The more in touch you are with your own internal world and frequency the easier it will be to notice when it starts to be impacted by external things.

What this means is to slow down, and ask yourself multiple times a day "what am I feeling?" and "what sensations am I aware of in my body right now?" and "what thoughts are contributing to what I am feeling right now?" As your consciousness increases, you become lighter and lighter and more and more able to make choices about what you want to think and feel rather than reacting unconsciously maybe in ways you don't like.

In addition to becoming more aware of what you are feeling and thinking, proactively finding ways to practice feeling good is very important in practicing vibrational alignment. This is unique for everyone. Some people like pickles, and some people like flowers for example in helping keep their vibration elevated. Making a list of things that bring you joy and bringing them into your life often is a great way to bring your frequency up.

Practicing bringing in positive thoughts all day long is also very important in staying in alignment. What makes you happy to think about? For some people it might be their sweet sweet golden retriever, or for others it may be thinking of a time they felt peaceful and relaxed on vacation at the ocean.

Positive affirmations are a nice way to give your brain something positive to do instead of vibrating in worry or fear energy. One of my absolute favorites is "Everything's always working out for me," from Abraham Hicks. Also "Only good will come from this," from Marilyn Jennett feels really nice, especially when something feels challenging.

Our thoughts create our feelings, so it's very important to shift negative thoughts and bring in positive ones all day long. It takes some time to shift patterns of thinking that you've had for a long time, so be patient with yourself and consistent about your practice. Remember it's like lifting weights, it takes time in the gym to build a bicep, and it takes time to practice new positive thoughts to build a new neural pathway in your brain.

There are so many reasons to focus on elevating your vibration. High frequency in the body keeps people healthy, and health problems move through faster if they do manifest. Your energy attracts your life circumstances. The happier and more full of light and positive energy you are, the more positive circumstances you will continue to manifest in your life.

For all of you lovely empaths who care so much about the world, it also helps others live their best lives as well. Living in high frequency consciously and unconsciously gives others around you to live in that way as well. It helps us all move forward and expand as we are meant to do.

Creating a positive energy field can be a fun thing to practice, some simple and quick ways to elevate your vibration are:

Practicing affirmations like the ones above, or "abundance is my divine right, I am healthy, wealthy and loved." Finding positive mantras to repeat periodically or finding time to focus on for 10-15 minutes at a time is a great way to stay feeling good.

Spending time visualizing things that bring your energy up. If you love your cat, spend time visualizing her precious little face when you're not together. If your house on the lake is your favorite thing, taking time often to create peaceful scenarios in your mind about you being there will help elevate your vibration.

Visualizing opening up the crown chakra on the top of your head and imagining beautiful sparkly white light pouring into it and flowing through your whole body. Feeling the positive energetic shifts from the light growing stronger and lifting your vibration up.

Hang out with cool people! Meaning powerful, positive and inspirational people. People that make you feel good and energized after being with them.

Get out in nature. Nature is way more intelligent than we are at maintaining a harmonious vibration, and surrounding yourself with this energy will help integrate this more into your body as well.

Remember appreciation. Shifting into the energy of appreciation is an instant way to feel good and shift your frequency. There are always things to be grateful for. Your health, your job, food, resources, family, etc.

Get active! Getting your body moving and blood pumping is another quick way to elevate your vibration. There are so many reasons why this is effective, but all you really need to know is it works!

Drink water. It sounds simple but again it just works. We are made of 70% water, and the more hydrated we are the better we feel and the easier it is for us to connect to the divinity inherent within us.

The biggest key to vibration elevation is knowing and believing that you have the power to do it.

You are powerful beyond measure and realizing this and practicing shifting your frequency can be one of the most meaningful things you do in your life.

It will help you bring more of your uniqueness into the world and continue to help the rest of humanity evolve as well. You were born to do this!

Journal Exercise #3

Write, in as much detail as you can, about the three most joyful experiences you have ever had. What did they feel like? Sound like? Look like?

the sensitive soul's guide to spiritual awakening

Please express to me what is in the highest good about creating more joy in my life.

Write a list of 20 things that bring you joy.

1. _____
2. _____
3. _____
4. _____
5. _____
6. _____
7. _____
8. _____
9. _____
10. _____
11. _____
12. _____
13. _____
14. _____
15. _____
16. _____
17. _____
18. _____
19. _____
20. _____

Schedule at least one thing from your joy list to have fun with every day.

practice:

Positive Love check ins throughout the day:

Set alarm for every hour, stop, put hand on heart and belly, take 5 deep breaths in through the nose, longer exhale sighing through the mouth, call to mind something that makes you very happy (maybe one of the three experiences you journaled about above) and stay in that energy for at least 30 seconds.

How joyful can you be? Practice all day long keeping your thoughts in a positive place.

Spend time cultivating a creative outlet to tap into the power of your second chakra and increase your joy.

affirmation:
"*My joyful energy expands every day!*"

energy tip:

Place hands on 2nd Chakra (below the belly button) multiple times a day and ask, "Does this bring me joy?"

Finding clarity on what brings you joy helps you recognize that feeling for your purpose.

chapter five

3rd Chakra
Self Love

3rd Chakra | Self Love

The third chakra represents immunity, your thoughts, and self-love.

Self-love is the foundation for connecting to your unique truth and trusting it to step into your true potential.

Sensitive, empathetic people usually have a harder time loving themselves and can easily love others.

This is really fear/ego holding you back from fulfilling your soul's mission on earth this time around.

Remind yourself that loving yourself is really the highest gift you can give to yourself and the world.

The more we all live in our own truth, the lighter and more loving the energy of the planet will become.

Our job as individuals is to bring in so much light and love to our bodies it ripples out to those around us as an inspiration and reminder to their energy systems of the truth as well.

What does self-love really mean? It's that feeling that no matter what happens, or what "mistakes" you think you have made, you are really perfect. That feeling of unconditional support and understanding that comes from someone that really sees you on a deeper level than anyone else. The feeling that you are all right, right now, no matter what.

Sometimes for sensitive people especially, it can feel that it may be egotistical or narcissistic to love ourselves. We are taught to love others, and put them first. We're taught to be humble and not prideful. We are told that being hard and critical of ourselves is the way to motivate and push ourselves forward in life. If we ease up or are actually kind to ourselves, maybe we won't continue to make progress or people will judge us for thinking we're better than them.

This way of thinking is totally backwards when it comes to the truth, co creating the life that you want, and living in the best and most collaborative way with the rest of the people on earth. What if everyone felt so loving towards themselves and in alignment that they could be generous with everyone else?

When we are hard on ourselves it actually creates fear in our bodies, which generates a feeling of needing to protect ourselves and compete with others, which creates separation and disconnection and inhibits our growth as individuals and collectively.

The ego wants us to believe this illusion of separation so that it can continue to have a job and run the show. If we realized how lovely and magnificent we all are and truly felt that love on a deep level, we really would never listen to the fear based ego and then it would have to retire.

If we started listening to the truth about ourselves instead, that we are all one, that there is no separation, that we are all unique expressions of divine love, we would lift ourselves up first and positively impact those around us and continue the evolution of the consciousness of the human race.

We are generally unaware of our inner dialogue and how negative it can be. In order to begin to shift the pattern of negative thoughts and feelings about ourselves that prevent self-love, we need to pay more attention to what we are thinking about. Once we start practicing more awareness of all of our thoughts, and setting the intention of being kinder to ourselves, the negative judgments will begin leaping to the surface for us to see and then begin to shift.

Generally the judgments may not feel terribly mean, things like "you could have done better" or "why did you do that" or "you should have known." This subtle version of negative self-talk can be easily justified as motivational perhaps, or as helpful critical feedback. Generally when we have received this sort of feedback growing up or throughout our life it is comfortable and easy to slip into this kind of dialogue with ourselves.

Sometimes it can be much harsher, and when practicing awareness this can be almost easier to spot because the emotional impact is stronger. For example "you stupid idiot" might be easier to become aware of than "you could have done better" because the way that thought makes us feel is more intense. All of it, however, subtle, clear, harsh, mean and negative has an impact on you, your feelings, and therefore the direction of your life.

Some gentler, kinder and more helpful for you in actually achieving your goals, ways of saying the same things are, "I'm proud of you for trying, here's what you can do differently next time" or "I can see why I did it that way, and here's the beautiful learning that came from that for the future" and "how could you have known? You've never done that before."

It can feel real silly at first if you've never practiced the inner dialogue of saying kind and loving things to yourself. That doesn't mean it's wrong or to stop however, it means you need it even more. Just remember that slight shifts to a more self-compassionate way of speaking to yourself make a huge difference in your vibration and energetic system.

The more and more sensitive and in touch with your emotions and body responses, the easier it is to use the clues to tune into any negative thoughts that are creating it. Starting to pay attention more of the time in general will help you become more aware of all of the inner dialogue, as well as using your body and feelings to guide you to when things are going down the negative road internally.

Some ways to connect to the power of self-love in everyday life are:

Start with awareness. Again, the more aware you can be of internal thoughts and feelings the easier it will be to shift from fear to love in the moment. As you become more aware of the old unconscious internal fear based dialogue and how it impacts how you feel energetically, your motivation for working on it will continue to increase.

Who doesn't want to feel good? As we become more conscious that we actually have a big impact on the way we feel by what we're telling ourselves, we start to notice the payoffs of doing it differently. More energy, feeling happier, and co creating a more delightful life in the future.

Proactively bringing in the good. While it's super important first of all to cultivate awareness of negative self-talk, what really creates lasting change in your neural networks and energetic system is the bringing in of the positive self-talk on purpose, all day every day.

For example, taking account of all the things you do in a day and being proud of yourself. Reminding yourself often of the things you love about yourself "I'm so loving," "I'm such a wonderful friend" "I really showed up for that person in my life today," for example.

If it's difficult for you to feel love towards yourself, spending time in meditation cultivating the feelings of love you have for someone/something you love deeply, and then transferring that feeling to yourself can be very effective. Whether that is your dog, your child, your mom or your best friend, most everyone knows what that feels like, and it's a good place to start practicing.

Another way to bridge the gap from feeling neutral or negative about yourself to loving yourself, is to spend time in meditation and throughout the day imagining loving light (or sparkles, or stardust, or rainbows, whatever works for you) surrounding and loving you. This is actually happening all the time whether you are aware of it or not, and reminding yourself of this more often will help the feeling grow and build the bridge between love from everything to love from and to yourself.

A helpful tool from Abraham Hicks is to repeat, over and over again for at least 5 minutes, a prayer of thank you to whatever your belief system aligns with for loving you so much. Something like "thank you for loving me, thank you for guiding me, thank you for adoring me, thank you for cherishing me, etc...." This will shift your energy very quickly and put you in the frequency of love.

A simple, quick tool to use often while working on self-love is to simply put your hand on your heart, taking some deep breaths, and imagining loving energy flowing in. This simple act produces oxytocin, the "love" hormone, the same one produced by nursing mothers to help bond with their child, and in loving relationships to connect people together. What a miracle that we are able to produce this same feeling simply by touching and loving ourselves!

There are so many benefits to working on loving yourself. Increased health, decreased stress, more ability to know what you want and to manifest it into your life, and more healthy and connected relationships just to name a few. All of earth school can be a helpful practice in loving yourself through it, have fun practicing on the journey!

What did you learn about self-love growing up?
Examples: Was it considered selfish or healthy to speak kindly about yourself?

_____

_____

_____

_____

_____

_____

_____

What beliefs are helping you feel more self-compassion, and what do you want to transform?

_____

_____

_____

_____

_____

_____

_____

_____

What is one affirmation, and one practice you can commit to every day?
Example: "I am learning to love myself more every day." And telling each body part how much you love it in the shower each day.

_____

_____

_____

practice:

Feel the love for those you love, hold onto that feeling and transfer this onto yourself. Savor it, and practice multiple times a day.

Bring in self-love language all day every day.

Practice speaking kindly to your self in the mirror.

Practice self-appreciation in the shower, brushing teeth, etc.

affirmation:

"I'm learning to love myself more every day."

energy tip:

The element of this chakra is fire. Walk outside in the sun for 20-30 minutes per day, if not possible, visualize the sun, feel its power radiating through your body. Allow this energy to light you up, helping remind you of your true power!

the sensitive soul's guide to spiritual awakening

chapter six

4th Chakra
Let Others
Voluntarily
Evolve

4th Chakra
Let Others Voluntarily Evolve

The fourth chakra represents unconditional love and compassion, as well as boundaries for an empathic person.

As an empathic person, you are naturally compassionate, loving and tend to worry about and help others. You have a beautifully expanded heart chakra because you care so deeply about humanity.

While these are lovely qualities, in order to continue your own personal spiritual awakening journey, it's important to remember to not over sacrifice or help others, and to take care of yourself.

To expand in the way you were meant to, you need to stay in your own lane. Change relationships in which you are doing more, listening more, caring more than the other person.

Fixing or worrying about others is so draining and blocks us from living to our highest potential. You are not responsible for anyone else's feelings or behavior.

When we give too much, we block our ability to receive. We must absorb lots of energy to keep our energy high to help ourselves and others.

The work of staying in your own lane, not worrying about others, or absorbing their energy is required to be able to help others do the same.

When we aren't channeling our healing gifts in a healthy way, we tend to do it to friends, partners, family members, etc. Who don't really need or want it usually.

L.O.V.E: Let others voluntarily Evolve. Everyone is on their own healing journey. Fixing and enabling others blocks them from being able to learn what they need to learn on a soul level to evolve how they really are meant to.

Letting others voluntarily evolve means to let go, and allow other people to grow in the way that's best for them, not how or when we think they should.

Have you ever thought to yourself "if they just understood, they would do it this way" or "why can't they just do it right?" There are many other examples of this way of thinking, but they all really come down to this: feeling like your way is the right way and other people should do things the way you want.

If you are an empath and a compassionate old soul you might feel frustrated a lot at others in your life that aren't the same way. You feel that you just can't understand the way they act or the things they say. Well the thing is, you don't need to understand, and trying to is just a waste of everyone's time and energy.

So many people stay in marriages, or relationships with friends or family members for far too long in the hopes that they will "get it." They wait for the other person to see the world the way they do, to expand their consciousness to the same level. This very often doesn't happen!

It doesn't mean you can't stay in relationships with these people, of course you can! It just means you need to shift from an expectation that they see things your way to an acceptance that they are wonderful just the way they are. Evolution is not a race, and love means accepting people for all of their uniqueness. Not wanting them to change or understand things the way you want them to.

If you find yourself around people often that frustrate you, or trying to figure out why they think about things the way they do, it's time to stop. Either stop hanging out with those people, or find a way to release your expectations.

Love is not trying to change someone. Love is not trying to figure out their motivations or analyze their actions. Love is not wishing someone was different than how they are right now.

Love is seeing the best in someone. Love is eternal patience with their soul evolution process. Love is letting go.
 Love is letting others voluntarily evolve. What does this mean? Everyone's soul is a different age, has different things to learn, and is on a different timeline. There is no race, there is no rush on this process of conscious evolution. No one can make someone else evolve. Until

the person is ready themselves, there is nothing someone can do or say that can make another person change their consciousness. We can plant seeds, and they may have some impact at some point, but waiting, and forcing, and being frustrated that they aren't blooming yet is not helpful for anyone.

It's not always easy to let go of the desire to change people. It makes so much sense to us what would help them. Conscious, compassionate people want the best for others. It can be hard to watch someone make mistakes when we can see so clearly what would help.

But, guess what? It's not our job! Helping too much makes the people in our lives annoyed with us and also takes away their opportunities to learn what they need to learn. When we put pressure on others to change, or just try to do the changing for them, they don't get to figure out what they actually need to work on to evolve. They don't have the incentive to do the inner work that their soul really wants them to do.

Us trying to "help" is really not helpful! If we can pull out, and take a higher perspective from a soul level, it's a little easier to let go. When we can remember that everyone's soul is in charge and trust that they are a powerful being, life goes much more smoothly for everyone.

This "help" also usually comes from a place of worry, fear, or projection from us lovely sensitive empaths. We falsely believe that if we are worried about someone, we should help them, and then things will get better.

The problem with this is that worry and fear energy never actually helps anyone. This actually sends negative energy to the person, and keeps them stuck. Their soul receives the message from us that "you aren't capable of taking care of this" and "you need my help." The person you are trying to help therefore ends up feeling less capable and more helpless. This doesn't help them grow. This doesn't help their evolution on a soul level. This keeps them stuck.

It also doesn't feel good to you either. Just start paying attention to your energy system when you are worried about someone and trying to help them. Feel your frequency shift when you feel the need for someone to change. Feel on a subtle level that this is draining your energy as well as theirs.

Now, try a different approach. Think of someone you think needs help. This person isn't doing things the way you think is right, and it is frustrating you. Instead of sending the energetic message of fear and worry,

the sensitive soul's guide to spiritual awakening

send them messages of love, wholeness and perfection.

Visualize them in perfect health and happiness, with the situation resolved in a beautiful way without focusing on the details. Remind both of your energy systems that they are a powerful soul on the perfect evolutionary journey for them, and they are right on track. Now just imagine how much more helpful this is for you, them, and the rest of humanity on an evolutionary level. Feel the difference in your body when you focus on light, healing and wholeness versus worry and fear. Notice the difference in the relationship with this person when they can feel that you have faith in their ability to take care of themselves. This is a lifelong practice. You will always care about and want the best for people of course. The practice of letting go is just a more effective, more evolved way of helping everyone, including yourself, live their best life while they are here on earth school.

Everyone is surrounded by love, light and help. You can let go and trust that everyone will be taken care of, there is nothing to fear!

Journal Exercise #5

Take an honest inventory of relationships in your life.

Ask yourself:
Am I giving more than they are?
Do they ask me questions about myself and my life?
Do I feel overly responsible for taking care of them or their feelings?

For any relationships you feel are out of balance for you, ask yourself:
Is this relationship healthy enough to work on saving?
If so, what boundaries do you need to set to bring it more into balance?
If not, how can you make the changes you need to create more space/end the relationship?

practice:

Start creating awareness of the moments you are worrying, fixing, helping too much.

Instead, slow down, visualize energy moving from your heart chakra into your lower chakras, wiggle your toes, and ask yourself "what am I feeling?"

Practicing tuning into yourself in these moments will help you from focusing too much on the feelings of others, which will drain your energy.

Once you are in your own body again, visualize all the cells of your body opening and absorbing high frequency light that helps you to feel light and joyful.

You are more able to help others when you keep your energy high!

Once you know how you feel and come back into your body and fill yourself up with beautiful energy, you can see their higher self more clearly.

Their soul knows that they are powerful, and capable of helping themselves!

Practice seeing them as whole, healthy, and capable, just as the universe sees them! Send positive energy to a positive outcome for them, and trust that all is working out for their highest good.

When you let go of the feeling of responsibility for others, it frees you up to absorb more energy, which helps you and everyone so much more.

affirmation:

"What if I easily receive all that I truly deserve?"

energy tip:

Visualize tons of light/energy/butterflies/sparkles flowing into the back of your heart chakra as you remind yourself that you are absorbing high frequency energy.

The back of the heart chakra has an enormous capacity to receive energy that will help you feel amazing, radiate light, and increase your positive vibration!

Empaths need to receive even more energy than they give out to help replenish all of the energy they give to the world!

chapter seven

5th Chakra
Speak Your
Truth

5th Chakra | Speak Your Truth

The 5th Chakra or throat chakra is about speaking your own personal, powerful truth into the world so that you can manifest what you really want.

The 5th chakra is the most powerful energy center in the body.

The 5th chakra is the most powerful energy center in the body. In order to continue your spiritual awakening journey, it's essential to uncover and speak your authentic truth.

Most empathic people have a hard time knowing and speaking their truth because they are:

• Too tuned into others feelings
• Worrying about hurting/disappointing others
• Not confident in their truth

It's really hard to express how you feel and what you want when you don't know how you feel and what you want. This is a big part of the problem that I encounter with clients that I work with on communication issues. They complain of not being listened to, or feeling nervous to bring things up to people in their lives. Some people understand why they feel this way. They know that they are disconnected with how they really feel, or have a fear of conflict, or many other reasons they can point to for not expressing themselves. Some people understand that this is a problem in their lives and want to work on it. Another group of people find nothing wrong with not expressing how they really feel and don't want to do anything to change it. "It works for me" they tell me.

Sometimes I am one of the only people in their lives that they are truly open with. I always feel privileged and honored to hold space for people in this way. I also encourage my clients to find their voice and use it in the other relationships in their lives.

So what's the problem with keeping things inside? What's wrong with going with the flow and not "rocking the boat" by being authentic? Well just so many things!

If we are not being honest about how we feel in all of the relationships in our lives: work, romantic, family and friends, these aren't real authentic relationships. If we are not speaking the truth, those we are in relationships don't really know us. They know the polite, "what do you want to do?", "oh that's fine with me" version of us. That's not who we really are.

There are many reasons why this pattern manifests for people. Often people who have trouble expressing themselves were in some way not seen or validated when expressing their feelings growing up. They tend to be highly empathic and sensitive, worrying more about the feelings and needs of others than their own. They value peace and harmony more than their own wants and needs, and will sacrifice what they want in order to preserve it. Often, people aren't even conscious of this pattern in their lives until it reaches a critical point. Empaths and sensitive people are highly skilled at feeling the feelings of others, and often have a lot of trouble being aware of how they truly feel. This can lead to living lives and being in relationships with people that don't really make them happy.

When the sparks of awareness that things need to change happen, this can begin the process of self-exploration. Understanding how you really feel can begin slowly and with conscious intention, or sometimes it happens by force, when a crisis of some kind comes in to wake you up to how you really feel.

For example: sometimes people start working on personal growth because they are just feeling a little off and not sure why. They take time and work on things to become clearer on their real feelings. Other times, something like a terrible review at work can be a catalyst to realizing that you never liked that job or career path at all. This can lead to exploration of feelings on other topics as well, and eventually changing things to become more in alignment with your real truth.

As the process of awareness increases, it becomes increasingly uncomfortable to not make some change. This includes having conversations you may feel challenged by, in order to continue your evolution.
The focus of this today is not the becoming aware of your feelings part. I have written about that elsewhere and will continue to in the future. This is about how to speak this new truth that you are starting to become aware of with the people in your life that need to hear it.

Some steps to practice speaking your authentic truth are:

Connecting with your true emotions:

Take many opportunities each day to slow down, take some deep breaths and ask yourself "what am I feeling?" It will take time and practice to know how you really feel, versus what your brain is telling you you are feeling.

Meditating and then journaling your feelings will help you connect with them more clearly. This helps you get out of your brain where fear and ego live, not your real emotions.
Your true emotions will be calm, and not associated with fear or anxiety.

For example: your brain might say "this job has great benefits, I like my coworkers, and it pays well." While your true feelings are something like "I feel trapped, this job is boring and soul sucking and I want to feel more fulfilled!"

Start with a sacred space:

Creating a safe container to begin the process of being vulnerable is very important. When beginning to stretch your authenticity muscles, you want to start in easy ways that will help to build your confidence.

Starting with someone that won't understand you, or will be defensive or invalidating will probably just feel discouraging and make you think it's not a good idea to continue.

Finding someone that you feel safe with to start practicing saying how you feel can help it feel easier. As you start expressing yourself with a dear kind friend, a therapist, or even your cat or a journal, you will start noticing how much lighter you feel.

As you speak your truth in safe spaces you will also begin to become more clear on more truths in your life and how and who to speak them to.

Practicing mindfulness in the moment:

When you have gotten some practice in knowing your true emotions, and expressing them to people that you feel safe with, it's now time to graduate and speak them to more challenging people in your life.

It could be your mother who always criticizes you, or maybe your boss who hasn't given you a raise in 5 years, or maybe your partner who really needs to help out more with the housework.

These more challenging situations probably have real reasons for feeling hard. Maybe you've tried saying how you feel and they don't listen, or maybe you feel like they would get mad at you.

Whether the fear is based on real history, or in your imagination, it produces the same chemical reaction in your body. It triggers the fight or flight response, which blocks our ability to feel our feelings and express them effectively.

It's very important in situations we feel triggered in, to stay present when we are in these conversations.

To do so, find ways to get into a good feeling place first. Meditating for a few minutes, taking some slow deep grounding breaths, noticing all of the sights and sounds around you, doing a body scan and other mindfulness practices can get you into your body and ready to have a conversation.

While you're in the conversation, remembering to breathe and feel your feet in your shoes can help you stay grounded.

Getting prepared:

If you have a habit of feeling nervous in challenging conversations, it is a good idea to actually write some notes down for yourself. You will be practicing mindfulness as well, so you will be calmer, but it's a good idea to bring in some notes so that you don't forget anything if you still are a little nervous.

Check your expectations. Meaning, don't have any. You asserting yourself and feeling good about it does not depend on how the other person responds. Go into it without an expectation of outcome, just an intention of showing up as you really are.

Checking in with the person beforehand and asking if it's a good time to talk. If it isn't, just follow up and set a date and time that will work for both of you.

Follow up:

Congratulate yourself, you are so awesome for challenging your old pattern! It's so important to celebrate your accomplishments as you begin to shift into more authenticity. It's not always easy to grow, so giving yourself a pat on the back will help continue to build your confidence.

Share your successes with your soul tribe. Success doesn't necessarily mean that your mom will stop criticizing you forever, or you immediately get a raise, or your partner starts doing all the housework. Success here means that you are stepping into a more powerful and authentic version of yourself by speaking your truth. Let your people celebrate with you!

Use the information that you are gathering in these new conversations to help give you information about the people in your life, and the direction you want to go in the future.

This means that if you are starting to know how you feel, and speak it in kind and authentic ways and the situations in your life are not feeling better, it may be time to look at changing them.

For example, if you continue to confidently and compassionately ask for a raise after 5 years, and it's still not happening.....start looking for a new job. Don't keep expecting things to change that aren't working for you. It's up to you to change yourself.

This is a super fun and exciting area to work on. In my experience, as I see people becoming more confident in saying what they need to say to the people they need to say it to, their lives just keep getting better and better...

Our words are our wands, they create our reality. Keeping your truth inside will keep you stuck inside an unfulfilled life. Life is about expansion, individually and collectively. Letting your truth out helps elevate the consciousness of everyone. Thank you for your help!

Ask yourself: "Where in my life am I speaking my truth, and how can I tell?"
Really feel into the answers, be honest with yourself, there are no right or wrong answers when you are learning about yourself!

Ask yourself: "What areas in my life are harder to speak my truth?"
Identify what they are, and identify the factors involved. Is it harder with certain people, or about certain topics, or generalized everywhere?

Be honest and kind to yourself, remind yourself your empathy is a gift, and that your truth from your sensitive perspective is a much-needed gift to the world.

_____

_____

_____

_____

_____

_____

_____

_____

_____

_____

_____

_____

_____

_____

_____

_____

_____

_____

_____

_____

_____

_____

_____

_____

_____

_____

Give your younger self some compassion.
Using some of what you learned about yourself from your root chakra exercise, you can have empathy for the child that learned how to shut down their own voice, give them compassion, and remind them that they are strong and safe, and it is necessary for them to speak their truth now.

practice:

Practice writing your true feelings, gaining clarity on them, then start speaking them out loud to your cat, or in your car, to get used to how it feels.

Then begin to expand this to people in your life that you trust, building your confidence.

As you start to embody the feeling of authenticity even more and notice the benefits, you will start to feel braver to speak your truth in more challenging situations, you can do it!

Give yourself love, compassion and empathy along the way, and remember there is no private good. When you authentically speak your truth, you benefit yourself as well as those around you.

affirmation:

"I easily express my powerful truth!"

energy tip:

Singing helps open the throat chakra and strengthen the vagus nerve. Sing it loud and proud to get that Chakra flowing!

Chanting mantras is another way to work on the throat chakra. There are many options on YouTube, find something that resonates with you and practice with guidance or on your own.

the sensitive soul's guide to spiritual awakening

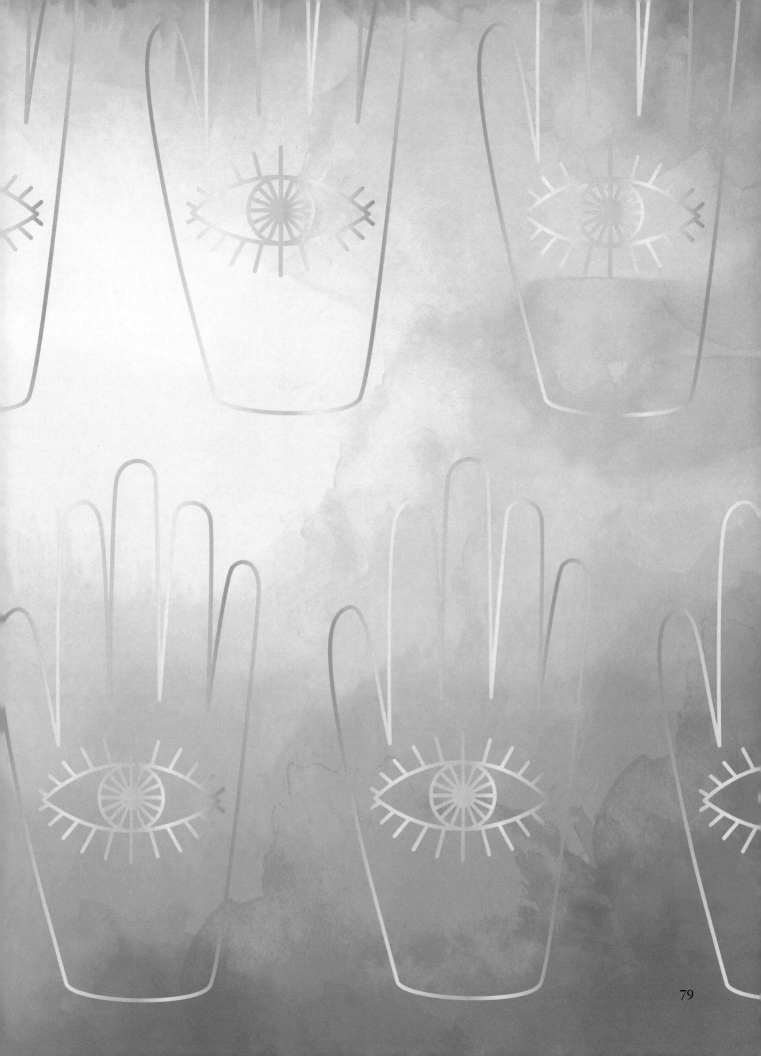

chapter eight

6th Chakra Your Intuitive Gifts

6th Chakra | Your Intuitive Gifts

The 6th Chakra is our third eye. This helps us see into the multisensory world, as we were designed to do.

Feeding your third eye with presence, self-love, and a calm nervous system is essential to be able to connect with your insight.

Empathic, sensitive people are often very intuitive, and tend to doubt their intuition.

Some reasons for not being able to hear and trust their intuition are:

Too worried about others:

Worry about others gets in the way of hearing intuition. Fear is our ego, and it blocks our intuition. Remember, L.O.V.E. and the 4th Chakra exercises to stay out of this vortex when listening to your intuition.

Tuning into others' emotions instead of themselves:

Empaths tend to feel others' feelings instead of their own intuition. Taking space away and tuning into ourselves is the only way to hear your intuition.

Self-Doubt:

Empaths are so kind to others but tend to be self-critical themselves. We can't hear or trust our intuition if we don't believe in ourselves. Practicing self love exercises from the 3rd Chakra will help this.

Overstimulated nervous system:

Sensitive people have a more easily stimulated nervous system. When it is activated in a stress response (fight, flight, freeze, fawn) we are disconnected from our intuition. Work on grounding exercises from the 1st Chakra work for this.

Not knowing what it sounds like:

It can be hard to tell the difference between thoughts and intuition. Intuition is calm, peaceful, loving, and gentle. Repetitive thoughts that keep coming back to nudge you in a positive direction.

Once you are more tuned into your higher wisdom, you will start to see it everywhere!

Pay attention, write about it, talk about it, get excited about it!

What is intuition and why is it important?

More and more people are understanding the importance of intuition and wanting to strengthen their own unique intuitive abilities.

In my view, intuition is the loving, positive, truthful, calm voice that we all have inside of us. This is the one that guides us towards our truth, our potential that we may or may not be aware of in a conscious way yet. The truth of our magnificence, that we tend to block with the fear or doubt of the logical mind much of the time.

I believe that this voice is the voice of source energy, where we all came from, what all life is made of.

Whatever your belief system is, whether this voice to you is your gut instinct, or your higher self, or God, or something different, you know what it sounds like and feels like.

Intuition sounds like:

Love
Calm
Positivity
Limitlessness
Encouragement

While we usually know what this feels like, many of us quickly tend to dismiss it, not believe it, or not even be aware of it because we are so busy, surrounded by others, or in our brains too much.

Our very sweet protective minds tend to come in and run the show most of the time. They tell us that they are super smart and strong, and if we don't listen to them there will be big trouble! Scary!

We don't want bad things to happen, so the tendency is to stay small and listen to the fear in order to stay safe and comfortable.

The voice of the logical mind, fear and ego sounds more like:

Fear
Doubt
Shoulds
Cant's
Limitation

Understanding the difference between the voice of your intuition versus your ego can simply be broken down by the feeling of love versus the feeling of fear. The feeling of expansion versus the feeling of contraction. Practicing feeling these differences and giving more power to the voice of love will help you continue to evolve in a positive and conscious way.

Why is this important? Well clearly to live a life without the integration of your own intuitive guidance is to live a life that is just not as rich, or beautiful, or positive, or fulfilling as it was meant to be!

We are born to remember this voice. All that happens to us is happening for us to connect back into this beautiful eternal voice of wisdom that has always been and always will be.

As we as individuals continue to work on this remembering, it helps the collective energy tune back into its own intuition as well. To remember that we are here to collaborate, not devastate, to love instead of hate, to be generous instead of holding on out of scarcity and fear.

We all need our intuition in order to make the best decisions for us in our own lives in areas such as love, career, family, and where we live just to name a few.

the sensitive soul's gu

Some simple and easy ways to practice connecting to your own internal wisdom are:

Practice getting out of your head consistently:

In order to hear your insight, it's imperative to practice quieting the mind.

Practice meditating consistently.

Practice being present and grounded consistently:

In addition to practicing meditation consistently (I do mean consistently!) placing checkpoints throughout the day to check in on your energy system is imperative to grow your connection with your intuition as well.

In the morning as soon as you wake up, practice feeling your energy system and do some grounding exercises.

A great way to practice presence is to spend about 30-60 seconds feeling the energy of your body and breathing energy and light into any areas that feel stagnant or need more life force energy flowing into them.

A favorite easy grounding exercise that I use all the time is to place your feet on the floor, sit quietly and imagine your feet growing roots into the earth. Imagine these roots pulling up beautiful earth energy into your feet and flowing up into filling your whole body with white light.

Throughout your day, put in checkpoints to remind yourself to practice presence and grounding. At least once an hour, put a reminder on your phone to check in and ground your lovely energy system.

Practice asking yourself intuitive questions:

An easy way to start is by picking between two choices.

For example, if you need groceries, get still, present and grounded.

Close your eyes and visualize two different choices of grocery stores. Feel into which of the choices feels more interesting, or alive, or sparkly to you.

Practice not listening to the voice of logic that might tell you to pick one option due to logical reasons (location, etc....).

Follow the intuitive guidance and take internal or external notes to help you validate your intuitive experience.

I had a fun example while doing this practice. My logical mind was telling me to go to Safeway because it was closer, maybe what I wanted would be cheaper, etc..... My intuition told me to go to QFC instead. I did this, they had organic celery on sale, and it happened that my dog who was at the vet (which was right next door to QFC) was able to be picked up earlier than expected, right after my grocery shopping. Amazing!

Starting with the small questions helps to build your confidence in your own intuition, in order to begin trusting it more with the bigger ones in your life!

Growing into intuitive awareness is like building a muscle. Be patient, kind and loving to yourself as you are growing into your practice.

Work on integrating these practices consistently takes time, I encourage you to dedicate time in building your skills here and gaining confidence in them before diving too deeply into the next steps.

These practices have many additional benefits, not just helping you to connect more to your intuition, but also helping you to feel calmer, more peaceful and in a higher vibration more of the time.

This is all laying the foundation for your awareness of new and more amazing possibilities for yourself to flow into your energy field.

As you continue practicing the basic skills over time of grounding and staying present, and start asking yourself easy questions, you should begin to feel a little more confident in discerning between your intuition and your mind.

This is not a race, it takes time to practice this, so be easy with yourself. If you're not all the way sure, every time, of what your intuition is telling you, remind yourself that this is normal. Remind yourself that you are growing in your insight every day and that you're doing a great job.

the sensitive soul's guide to spiritual awakening

Pay attention to when you are grounded and present. Congratulate yourself on increasing your ability to be in your body, sensing what is happening around you. Even though this sounds easy, it's not. It can be difficult to feel present and grounded, especially in challenging circumstances and when so many people are not feeling that way.

So notice, and stay in the moment when you are there. Remind yourself what a beautiful job you are doing in your practice of noticing your insight.

Being kind and loving to yourself increases your ability to hear your intuition:

Notice when you are grounded and present and savor the moment.

Pay attention when you are connected to your intuition and give yourself an internal (or external!) round of applause.

Your soul is so excited about the connection you are building with it. Remind yourself of how exciting this is and get excited too!

The more proud, and happy, and excited you can be about your growing abilities, the more they will continue to expand in your life!

As your confidence builds, expand your self inquiry:

We tend to block or run away from the bigger questions in our lives, especially if we already intuitively know the answer but are terrified to hear it!

For example, it's easy to ask ourselves what should be for dinner tonight, but can be much more difficult to ask things like "Am I truly still in love with my husband?" or "Why do I feel so bored and unfulfilled in my really high paying job?"

These bigger questions are where your soul and intuition get really excited, and the ego acts up and tries to block us from even asking the questions, let alone hearing the answers.

The ego says things like "You don't even have time to meditate, you have work to do!" and "Who do you think you are to not be happy, look how good your life is!"

It's your job to look past this fear and practice tuning in again to that sweet calmer quieter voice internally that knows what's best for you even though it might be scary.

When you ask the harder questions, remember that you have free will!

Remind yourself, just because you hear intuitive guidance doesn't mean you have to follow it.

Listen to the answers though. If you can hear the voice that is just asking you to explore the idea of exploring new ideas, this helps the intuition flow, and will allow new insight to flow through.

If you stay in fear, and don't let yourself hear your guidance, you block the flow of insight coming into your life.

This can be fun to practice in meditation. Begin by relaxing your body, remind yourself you are safe and have free will, and then gently float in a question that feels a little scary.

Just begin noticing any feelings, thoughts or images without judgment.

Remind yourself that you have free will, you get to do whatever you want. Even if your intuition is guiding you towards big changes, you don't have to listen.

Reminding yourself that you are in charge reduces the fear, allowing the answers to come through more easily.

You generally will end up following your intuition but reminding yourself you don't have to can increase your feeling of empowerment and allow your insight to be more clear.

Continue this practice consistently until your energy is calibrated to the knowing that any answer is ok, there is no wrong or right, and anything is possible, because it is!

Pay attention to the signs:

As your confidence and trust in yourself and your guidance grows, it becomes easier and easier to recognize what it has been trying to tell you all along.

You become more able to hear, see, and feel

the signs that have been there all along, guiding you along your path.

Ask for signs to help guide and validate the direction your guidance system is directing you towards.

True signs from your intuition will feel good, inspiring, peaceful and positive,

"Signs" that are not really signs, from your ego or fear feel scary, tense, stressful and limiting.

These signs are happening all the time, but there are some ways to make them clearer and more easily recognizable with conscious intention.

An example can be asking for signs about moving to California or not.

If you start seeing California license plates more, or meet someone new from California,

or have a dream about being on the beach in California.

These are signs to explore that direction more.

If you start fearing how much more expensive it might be, or worrying about how global warming will make it too hot to live there soon, or how lonely or scared you might be in a new place.

These are signs that you are limiting yourself with fear, that is not your intuition.

This is not linear, all cases are different, and again it takes time and practice to gain clarity. Intuition is subtle, and soft and gentle. This lovely voice is different than the harsher and louder voice of the mind and ego.

It is a lifetime practice to get to know yourself and your truth. I hope you have fun and enjoy the way your life unfolds when you are in tune with your own unique wisdom!

Journal Exercise #7

Write down three times in your life that you can remember clearly hearing your intuition.

What did it feel like? How could you tell it was your intuition and not something else? Did you listen to it or not?

_____

_____

_____

_____

_____

_____

_____

_____

_____

_____

_____

_____

_____

_____

It is valuable to remember that you are a powerfully intuitive being, as we all are. We are born to connect to our inner wisdom!

Keep an intuition journal:

Find a beautiful journal

Start practicing writing down intuitive messages

Start writing down synchronicities and signs you see around you.

Start building an intuitive dictionary for yourself, of signs and symbols that have unique meaning for you.

Practice tuning into someone's energy and writing down your impressions, and check out how accurate you are

practice:

Practice being present, in your body, and in a high vibration to be able to hear your intuition most clearly.

Remind yourself "I am a magically intuitive being, it's natural to hear my intuition!"

Start small. Take a deep breath and start experimenting with the different feeling of your intuitive voice.

Ask yourself an easy question, and feel into the thoughts, feelings, and sensations in your body and allow them to help you know the answer.

Everyone's intuitive process is different.

Automatic writing can bypass the ego mind and get you in touch with your intuition.

Quiet your mind and write down on the top of a piece of paper "Please express to me what's in my highest good about___

affirmation:

"I'm so grateful for the amazing power of my intuition!"

energy tip:

Practice rolling your eyes up as if you are looking at your third eye. Practice seeing your third eye in your mind's eye when asking an intuitive question.

This helps you focus and expand your intuition.

chapter nine

7th Chakra Your Spiritual Truth

93

7th Chakra | Your Spiritual Truth

The 7th Chakra is about our connection with divine source energy, trusting that the Universe has our back.

Empaths are uniquely able to feel this connection, and yet their sensitivity can create blockages in this chakra and mistrust of the universe as well.

Hypervigilance, fear can block our access to this amazing, blissful feeling of connection with the divine that we are meant to feel all the time!

Maintaining your spiritual connection daily is key to continuing to hear your truth

When you stay connected and aligned to this magic, you will be able to manifest it with this universal source of support

Remembering the bigger picture, that you are loved and adored beyond measure, and this is all here for you to expand your consciousness will help you stay on track and excited for your path to continue and expand

We are here to become as conscious as possible to help others to do the same

If you remain consistent in your practice, you will stay connected

It's never a one time (clearing, healing, release, etc...) Anyone that tries to tell you that has more of their own work to do

It is a lifelong practice of discovery, of healing yourself to heal others of awakening more and more consciousness to expand and help others as well

We are one. One with trees, one with stars, and one with each other. We are all made of the same stuff and are interconnected in a beautifully harmonious way.

Our soul knows this, and the feeling is undeniable and unforgettable. We were born with this understanding, and over time if we are not consciously practicing remembering it, it can feel like separation is real instead of connection.

We were designed to feel connected. Humans have never been meant to live in isolation, separation or conflict. We are meant to collaborate, and to harmonize in order to help ourselves and the collective survive and thrive.

Especially right now, as our country feels so divided, it's more important than ever, whatever side you're on, and whatever you believe, to practice remembering that we are more alike than we are different. That there is something bigger at work and working at connection and collaboration feels so much better to all involved and helps us all evolve and expand.

It's always so nice when science backs up things that sometimes feel "woo woo" or too subtle to understand. I'm sure most of you have felt the experience of oneness. Whether it was staring at the wonder of the Grand Canyon, or the Pacific Ocean, or a beautiful church service, or the innocent beauty of a newborn child.

It's that feeling of connection, of magic, of bliss that is the key to all of our continued growth and evolution. The more we can tap into this feeling, the higher our vibration becomes, allowing our energy to expand, and to help others expand as well.

The science that I'm talking about, is research on a part of the brain that shifts during a "spiritual" or "higher consciousness" experience. Research on experienced meditators and distance healing practitioners shows shifts in many areas of the brain during these kinds of experiences, but the most significant was in the parietal cortex, specifically the left inferior parietal lobule.

This part of the brain is activated when a person becomes aware of himself or others. When in meditation or focusing on sending healing energy or prayer to another person, or other forms of feeling connected to all that is, there is a reduction in activity in this section of the brain.

We all know how much better it feels to be in the energy of love instead of fear, and expansion instead of contraction. It's also validating to know the scientific explanations behind this. It's really happening, y'all, you really can change your brain with what you focus on, so cool!

The more of us that can be focusing on this, on purpose, the more our world can evolve and ascend into the light. It feels really good to be in this energy, it helps your life improve, and gives you the energy to expand your light even more brightly into the world.

We can train our brains to be in this place more often, some practical ways to practice feeling this oneness are:

Sending Loving Energy:

Research has shown that individually, or in a group, setting an intention to send love, healing energy, prayer, whatever you want to call it, to another person or group of people diminishes the activity in the parietal cortex.

If you have ever tried this you know how good it feels to hold loving energy for others. It helps improve your energy and that of those you are helping as well.

It can be fun to form a group and do virtual healing sessions for others, or you can practice just setting an intention to send this loving energy to others on your own.

It's easy to practice. Just relax your body in meditation, imagine who you are intending to send energy to, and focus on sending positive energy to them. There is no right or wrong way, have fun with your practice!

the sensitive soul's guide to spiritual awakening

Meditation:

We need to be able to still our minds in order to feel this connection.

This is the foundation, to connect to the stillness and truth that we are all one, we have to practice diminishing the other noise inside your beautiful brain.

Practice meditation to still your mind, and then expand into imagining your aura expanding, and your identity releasing.

You are one with the universe. There is no separation. Practice remembering this as much as you can.

This connected feeling is needed on earth now more than ever. We can all be part of the awakening of consciousness and helping to expand the light!

Experience the Magic of Nature:

The more we can help our energy systems remember the connection we have with the natural world, the better we feel.

We are designed to be close to nature and feel its rhythms often, in order to align our own energetic vibration to the earth's energy.

Take some time, as often as you can, to set your intention to feel a communion with nature. Put your hand on a tree while on a walk and feel its peaceful energy. Sit by the water and feel how its gentle flow is connected to your own physical being that is also 70% water.

Practice experimenting with this connection with nature to help your brain and body remember this connection, and to help your energy system remind those around you of the truth as well.

Journal Exercise #8

What do you believe about the Universe? What did you grow up believing about God, faith, and a connection to something bigger than yourself?

Be honest with yourself about your beliefs, there are no wrong or right answers here.

the sensitive soul's guide to spiritual awakening

What beliefs do you resonate with now?

Journal your beliefs into existence, write down how you will be practicing integrating spiritual connection practice into your everyday life so that you can feel this divine connection every day.

What are three things you can commit do every day to remind your energy system that you are loved, surrounded, protected, and guided at every moment?

Examples:
Sitting for 5 minutes in the morning, absorbing the sunshine into your pores, reminding yourself that divine source energy is flowing into you. Meditation helps you connect with the Universe
Reading a spiritual text that inspires you.

practice:

Reading or listening to spiritual texts that you resonate with is a great way to remind yourself of the truth.

Empaths need quiet to hear the Universe and feel their spiritual connection.

Connecting to spirit is just so much easier and more fun in nature, so why not do that as much as you can?

Meditation is so important, so that you can increase your ability to be present, where all the magical connection to the Universe is!

Spiritual community is so helpful to maintain your feeling of connection to the divine.

Training your mind is necessary to maintain a feeling of connection to source and your intuition. Practice noticing negative thinking from the Ego and bringing in more positive thoughts.

Practice seeing life as something you chose to expand and evolve. Every moment is here to help us become more present and expand our consciousness!

Taking frequent breaks to tune into the bigger truth/connect to Universal truth. Reawakening moments throughout the day.

Say thank you, frequently, to the Universe for helping you, energizing you, guiding you, etc. This heightens your frequency and brings you even more into alignment with your higher self.

affirmation:

"I am one with the Universe."

energy tip:

Visualize opening your crown chakra on the top of your head and see enormous quantities of light flowing in throughout the day.

chapter ten

Integration After Awakening

A spiritual awakening is such a profound experience. It changes everything about the way you see yourself and the world around you. It's transformative, and amazing and magical.

It can also be confusing, and lead us to question many areas of our lives that previously felt ok. Maybe a job that was paying the bills and offering great health insurance used to feel like a comfortable way to spend your days. After your awakening, though, it may start to feel boring, or unfulfilling in a way that you were never aware of before.

Maybe a relationship or marriage that felt harmonious and easy before your internal changes now feels uncomfortable. Like you don't understand each other anymore. Like you'd really like them to just "get" how you now see the world but they don't.

Sometimes no one in your life understands. Just because we start to become more aware and see the world differently doesn't mean the people around us are going through the same thing. Depending on your family or community, you may be the first and only one to wake up. This can feel lonely and confusing sometimes. It doesn't mean you're on the wrong track. It doesn't mean to stop learning and exploring your spiritual path. It just means you are becoming more conscious, which is a beautiful thing.

As we awaken and become more aware of our connection to the universe and the fact that we are only love and create our own reality, things in our life naturally change. Just as it wouldn't make any sense for a butterfly to live under a leaf like a caterpillar, it also doesn't make any sense for an awakened soul to live the same way as someone more unconscious. Change is a natural part of the process of spiritual evolution.

If you feel that you are starting to awaken to a new way of being in the world, congratulations! You are here to assist in the conscious evolution of humanity. You are uncovering your brilliant light in order to increase the vibration of yourself and those around you.

This feels so exciting and amazing! At the same time, if you don't have some guidance along the way, the way to move forward and integrate your new awareness's into your current life can feel unclear.

I have gone through this process myself, and have also guided many others along the same journey. I know how it feels, and I know what has helped.

Some ways to recognize when you are transforming in your life are:

You are interested in things you didn't understand before:

You may start reading self-help or spirituality books.

You may be more interested in topics like psychology, energy healing, intuition, etc...

You might start practicing yoga or meditation.

You start feeling differently than "old you" did:

You see things with more love, forgiveness and compassion.

You become more sensitive to your environment.

You want and need more quiet introspective time.

You speak with more kindness and let go of resentments and grudges.

You crave connection, meaning and fulfillment. Superficial things and relationships don't matter to you anymore.

You collaborate instead of compete.

You become more aware of your intuition, and listen to it more than your fear based thoughts.

Some tips on how to move through the after awakening process with grace are:

Find like-minded people to talk to:

If you are in a space where you don't have anyone around you that understands the new you, find a trusted guide: a therapist who understands spirituality, an intuitive guide, an energy worker, or someone else you feel safe with to process and explore who you are becoming.

As you grow into the person you are becoming it is so important to find a soul tribe who is on

your new wavelength with you. You may already know these people, or you may get to go and explore and find them. As you awaken you will want to find people who are positive, compassionate and evolved to help continue your growth together.

You can find them in places that also can help you grow: a spiritual class, workshop or meetup, a church that resonates with you, yoga or meditation classes, or many other places depending on you and your unique path.

Finding ways to continue supporting yourself on your journey:

As you awaken and uncover more and more of who you truly are, you get to spend a lot of time finding the things that help to bring you joy and connection to yourself. And doing them, consistently! This helps keep your energy high and helps you stay spiritually connected.

With your new increased sensitivity and multi-sensory ability you are much more attuned to the things that truly bring you joy as well as the things that deplete you. It also becomes more difficult to continue activities or relationships that don't contribute to your evolution. Your soul just won't let you anymore!

So, tuning into those things that bring you joy

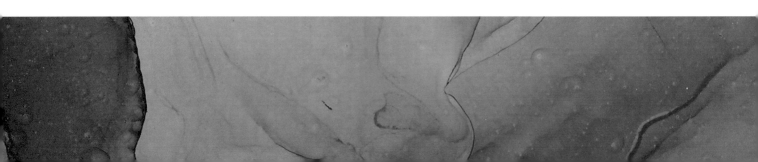

and spiritual connection, and bringing them into your life everyday will help you in the maintenance process after your spiritual awakening. It is like preventative medicine, keeping you alive, vital and connected. It is so important.

Some of the things that have helped me and those I have seen on their journeys are: journaling, meditating, being in nature, connecting with like minded people, reading inspiring things, practicing gratitude, yoga and many many other practices that are unique to every person.

Letting go of what no longer serves you: This doesn't have to happen all at once. Your new being will have new awarenesses. It's ok and necessary to just be with these new insights for some time before taking action on them.

It's easier now to listen to your intuition, which was really trying to get your attention for quite some time before you woke up. Just listen to it without shutting it down, even if you're not quite ready to leave the job or marriage yet, for instance.

Being aware of what your soul really wants is a huge accomplishment! We all have a lot of fear and defense mechanisms in place that can block us from hearing our own insight. Continuing to meditate and practicing connecting to your internal world is vital to stay in touch with what is true for you now and in the future. Taking time to process your new awarenesses internally, by journaling or other means can be helpful before sharing. When you're ready to open up to someone safe and loving in your circle, it can really help to gain support in moving forward with letting things go.

Take your time and be smart about it. If you are thinking of leaving a marriage or relationship, get some help for yourself from a guide or therapist, and also definitely do some work in couple's therapy before making any decisions. Before leaving a job, begin to get clearer on what would really make you happy before you quit just to get into another similar situation.

This isn't about making sudden rash moves to disrupt your life. It is about gently shifting your life more into alignment with your soul. That is when you will feel truly happy and at peace.

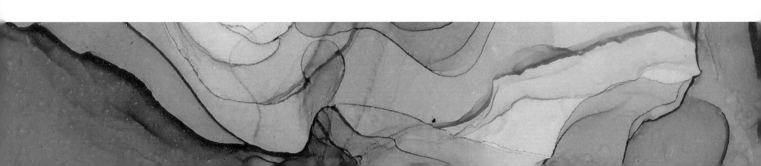

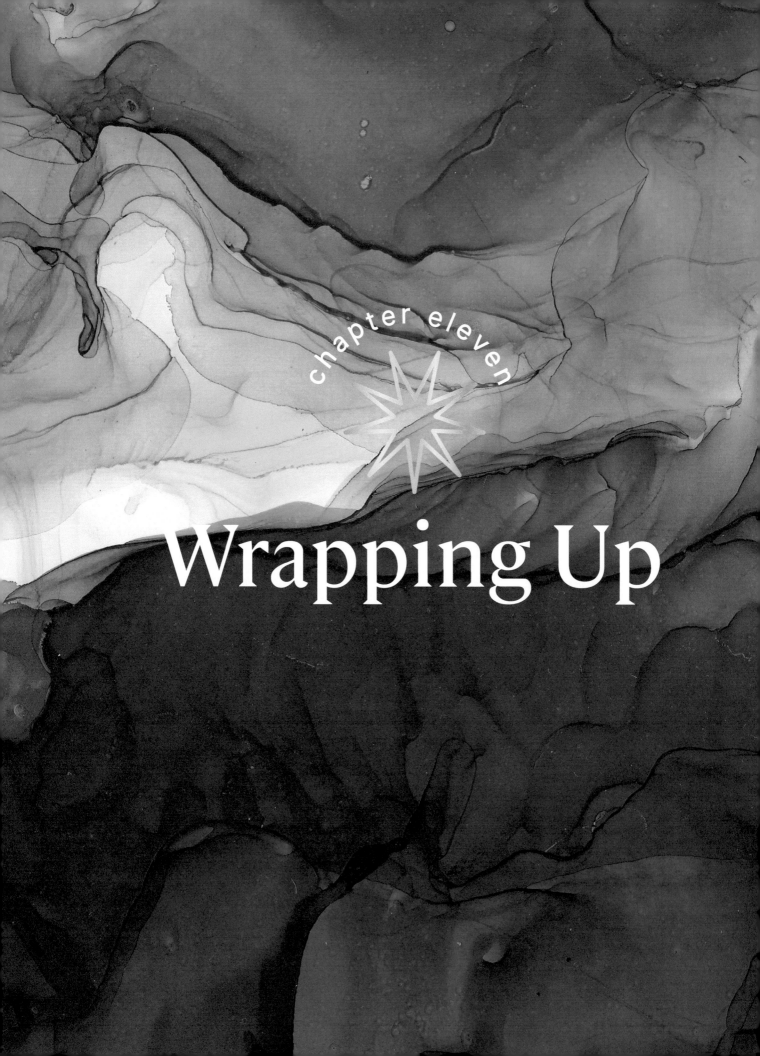

chapter eleven

Wrapping Up

My hope for you with this guide is that you feel a little closer to understanding yourself and your patterns. That you are feeling closer to the light, and understanding that you have always been and will always be a spiritual being. That you are here to expand in your consciousness, live in joy and have fun!

Life is a journey of self discovery, every moment is here to help you learn and grow. I hope this will be a tool for you along the way.

Moving through the Chakra system can be a visual representation of moving through a spiritual awakening. When we start from the foundational level, we are building a strong spiritual connection that will last and help you feel aligned and magical forever.

Creating awareness of old patterns, and a feeling of safety in our bodies is an essential first step to move towards spiritual connection. If we aren't grounded, our crown chakra can't recieve all the beautiful light it's capable of as easily!

As we feel safer, it becomes easier to feel the feelings we have in our bodies, and the joy that is really our natural state, our birthright to feel!

As our safety and joy increase, we find it easier to think more positively and love ourselves more. We are building the foundation for a beautiful spiritual connection.

The self love that we have worked on helps us remember to stay out of being in too much empathy for others. We learn to let others voluntarily evolve, and trust that everyone else is on their own spiritual journey as well, whether they are conscious of it or not.

Becoming more neutral in our heart chakra allows us to worry less about others feelings and speak our truth more powerfully into the world. Our throat chakra is where we hold our personal power, and how we manifest what we want in our lives!

All the work on our lower chakras prepares our energy system for the fun 6th vortex, our intuitive sense. As we heal, feel safe and joyful, and get out of other people's energy, we are able to really tune into our own intuition, and learn incredible insights about ourself and what we really want!

The foundation is now set for really feeling the beautiful spiritual connection through your crown chakra that you were born to have! It has always been there, there's just been too much in the way for you to feel it.

The integration of this work is a lifetime process, and these steps are a good groundwork to get started, and be able to come back to remind your energy system of any time you need it!

Made in The USA
Kirkland, WA
20 Oct 2022

Made in United States
Troutdale, OR
12/26/2023

16411604R00067